LOOK AND FIND

CARTOON NETWORK®

THE POWERPUFF GIRLS™

Illustrated by Animagination, Inc.
Written by Lynne Suesse

Based on "THE POWERPUFF GIRLS,"
as created by Craig McCracken.

Published by
Louis Weber, C.E.O.
Publications International, Ltd.
7373 North Cicero Avenue
Lincolnwood, Illinois 60712

www.pubint.com

Look and Find is a registered trademark of
Publications International, Ltd.

Manufactured in China.

8 7 6 5 4 3 2 1

ISBN 0-7853-4866-2

Publications International, Ltd.

W9-BGG-122

The City of Townsville!
And what a beautiful city it is. It's too bad that the Gangreen Gang is up to no good, placing phony phone calls and giving the Powerpuff Girls the runaround! None of the innocent citizens of Townsville can rest while these telephonies are using the telephone for their childish games. You can help! Find the Powerpuff Girls and these citizens who have fallen victim to the gang's pitiful pranks.

Blossom

Buttercup

Bubbles

MoJo JoJo

Fuzzy Lumpkins

The Mayor

Professor Utonium

SPOKEN IV

SUBS 'R US

TOWNSVILLE MALL

VISIT OUR OTHER STORES SPOKEN I, II, AND III

BANK

The City of Townsville!
And what a city it is... or was.
It seems giant fish monsters have
emerged from the lake at Bonsai
Gardens and are destroying this
fine city. The Powerpuff Girls have
tried to stop them, but they need
the help of Professor Utonium's
latest invention, Powerpuff Dynamo!
Yes, this calls for the first (and last)
Dynamic Nanotechtronic Monobot
that Townsville has ever seen. Help
the Powerpuff Girls find the fish
monsters lurking throughout
the city before it is gone for good!

Giant Fish Monster   Carpe Diem

Fish Wishy   Femme Fish

Fishy Business   Stink Fish

The Fishinator   Fish and Chips

FOOD   CAFFEINE ME!   COFFEE

MUSEUM

CANDY

BANK

Pattie's

Bonsai
Gardens

PokeyOaks
Kindergarten

The City of Townsville!
It's a dog day afternoon... literally. The evil Mojo Jojo has turned the quiet citizens of Townsville into dogs! During the night, Mojo Jojo stole the Anubial Jewels and the Anubis Dog Head statue from the museum, and now the whole town, the Mayor, and Professor Utonium have become dogs! Even the Powerpuff Girls are now Powerpups! Help catch Mojo Jojo by finding each of the Powerpups and more stolen jewels that will lead you to this evil villain. Then find the Mayor, Professor Utonium, and these other unfortunate citizens who have been dogified:

Blossom

Bubbles

Buttercup

These jewels

Ms. Bellum

The Mayor

Professor Utonium

Mr. Curator

Ms. Keane

BALLOONS

The City of Townsville! But wait! Color me troubled! The once vibrant and colorful community of Townsville is turning black and white! Rainbow the Clown turned into the evil Mr. Mime after a dangerous dose of bleach took away his colors. Now he wants everything stripped of color–even the Powerpuff Girls. Help capture this evil villain, find these helpless victims, and Bubbles' crayons to return Townsville to its rightful colors:

Bubbles

Blossom

Buttercup

Mr. Mime

Professor Utonium

Tommy Two-Tone

Sally Spectrum

Bubbles' Crayons

FLOWE

The City of Townsville!
Buttercup was temporarily taken by the charm and charisma of Ace, the leader of the Gangreen Gang. But when she finds out that he's planning to hurt Bubbles and Blossom, she's back to her old self and ready for a fight. Look around the Townsville Dump where the Gangreen Gang likes to hang out. Find Buttercup, then help her find all the members of the gang and her two sisters, who are being held captive.

Ace

Big Billy

Snake

Little Arturo

Bubbles

Grubber

Buttercup

Blossom

The City of Townsville!

Oh, no! A "cat"astrophe has befallen Townsville! After hypnotizing Professor Utonium, making him build a hypnotic modulator, and convincing him to steal the Cat's-Eye Jewel from the museum, the cutest, fluffiest...uh, I mean the most sinister, evil kitty to dig its claws into the shin of Townsville is hypnotizing its citizens and forcing them to become slaves to their cats. Help the Powerpuff Girls to save the day by finding that wicked kitty, the Cat's-Eye Jewel, and these cats who are making mischief with their new owners:

Evil Kitty   Cat's-Eye Jewel   Leche

Stinky   Scratches   Ju-Ju

Stealth   Nipsy

PETS

1123

NO DOGS ALLOWED

FRESH FISH

FRESH FISH

The City of Townsville is under attack! The most evil and sinister of all the villains has taken over Bubble's stuffed octopus and created trouble for the Powerpuff Girls. Now the giant octopus is out to destroy the world—and Townsville is its first target! Can the girls stop fighting each other and start fighting the evil Octi? You can help! Find these troubled citizens while the Powerpuff Girls work out their problems:

Blossom

Buttercup

Bubbles

S. Yuvee

Hugh Hal

Wendy Ryder

Doug E. Ketcher

Della V. Reed

Vandy Randy

Rusty Chopper

DOG CATCHER

HAUL-IT MOVERS

We cover the bottom line

The City of Townsville is hot! And it's no wonder—a giant fireball is racing toward the earth! As the temperature gets hotter, the children at the Pokey Oaks Kindergarten get crankier. Blossom uses her ice breath to cool down the class before she, Buttercup, and Bubbles save Townsville from a fiery fate. Look around the Pokey Oaks playground to find these cool kids:

Floyd and Lloyd

Julie Bean

Ms. Keane

Statue of Ms. Keane

Harry Pitt

Elmer Sglue

Mitch Mitchellson

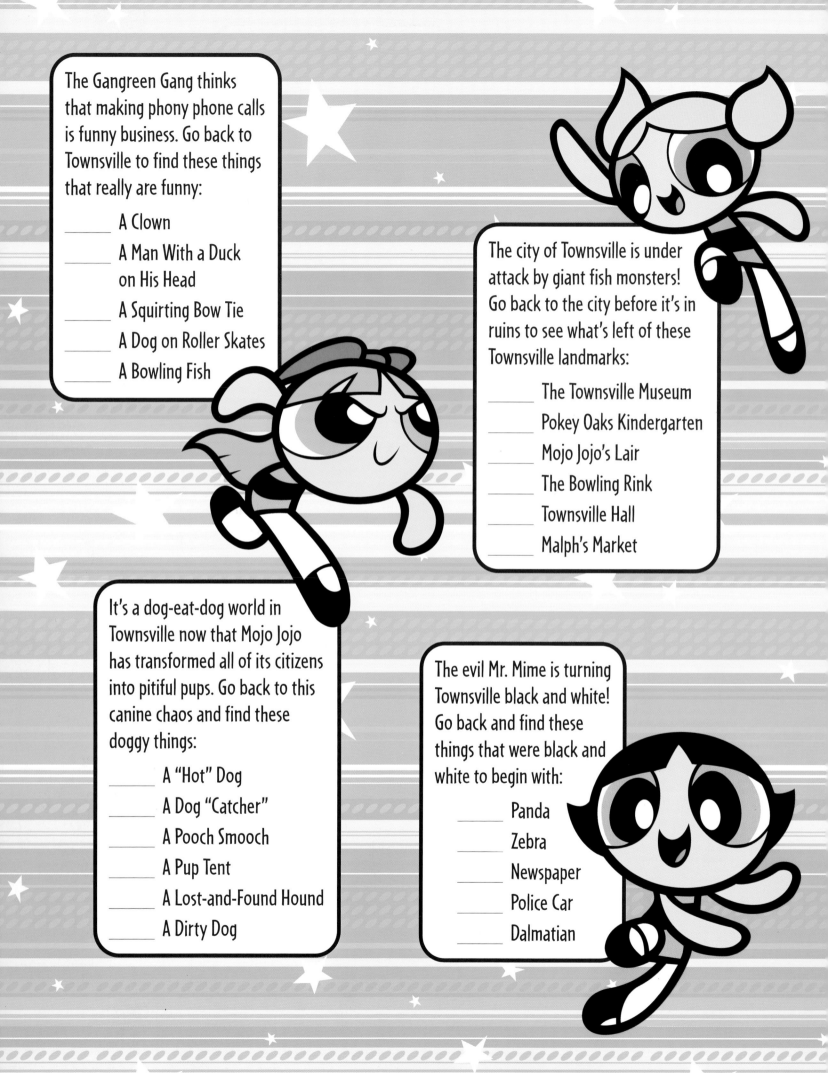

The Gangreen Gang thinks that making phony phone calls is funny business. Go back to Townsville to find these things that really are funny:

_____ A Clown

_____ A Man With a Duck on His Head

_____ A Squirting Bow Tie

_____ A Dog on Roller Skates

_____ A Bowling Fish

The city of Townsville is under attack by giant fish monsters! Go back to the city before it's in ruins to see what's left of these Townsville landmarks:

_____ The Townsville Museum

_____ Pokey Oaks Kindergarten

_____ Mojo Jojo's Lair

_____ The Bowling Rink

_____ Townsville Hall

_____ Malph's Market

It's a dog-eat-dog world in Townsville now that Mojo Jojo has transformed all of its citizens into pitiful pups. Go back to this canine chaos and find these doggy things:

_____ A "Hot" Dog

_____ A Dog "Catcher"

_____ A Pooch Smooch

_____ A Pup Tent

_____ A Lost-and-Found Hound

_____ A Dirty Dog

The evil Mr. Mime is turning Townsville black and white! Go back and find these things that were black and white to begin with:

_____ Panda

_____ Zebra

_____ Newspaper

_____ Police Car

_____ Dalmatian

While Buttercup is busy cleaning up the trash at the Townsville Dump, you can help. Go back to the dump and find these things that weren't meant to be thrown away:

_____ Stereo Speaker

_____ Torn Jeans

_____ Playing Cards

_____ Doghouse

_____ Old Mattress

_____ Newspaper

Don't take a catnap! There's more to be done. Cats are ruling Townsville, thanks to that evil hypnotizing kitty! Go back and find these very catty things:

_____ Cata"log"

_____ "Bureau"cat

_____ "Cat"amaran

_____ Cata"comb"

_____ Cata"list"

_____ "Cat"apult

It's no business like snow business at the Pokey Oaks Kindergarten, thanks to Blossom's ice breath. "Snow" back to the playground to find these snowy things:

_____ Snowman

_____ Snow "Globe"

_____ Snowy Owl

_____ Snow "Shoe"

_____ Snow "Crab"

_____ Snow "Bank"

_____ Snow Cone

The giant evil octopus that is threatening Townsville has caused quite a traffic jam! Go back to the troubled traffic and find these other jams:

_____ Raspberry Jam

_____ Toe Jam

_____ "Jam"boree

_____ A Jam Session

_____ A Paper Jam